COOKIE
COUNT & BAKE

A COOKBOOK AND CUTTER SET

BY DEBORA PEARSON

ILLUSTRATED BY JANE KURISU

Dutton Children's Books
New York

For Thomas and Taline—DP
To Lawrence—JK
To Alexandra and Miller — CCW

Acknowledgements: Many thanks to Nancy Moore, mathematics consultant, and Ellen Austrom, recipe tester, who also suggested the edible "paint" recipe. And special thanks to editor Jennifer Glossop, who skillfully mixed and measured words and helped serve up a delicious book!

Library of Congress Cataloging-in-Publication Data
Pearson, Debora.
Cookie count & bake: a cookbook and cutter set / by Debora Pearson; illustrated by Jane Kurisu.
—1st ed.   p.   cm.
Summary: Activities and recipes that illustrate concepts about numbers and geometric shapes.
ISBN 0-525-45694-5
1. Counting—Juvenile literature.   2. Cookies—Juvenile literature   [1. Counting. 2. Cookies.]
I. Kirusu, Jane, date.   ill. II. Title.
QA133.P43   1996   793.7'4—dc20   96-15414   CIP   AC

Published in the United States 1996
by Dutton Children's Books,
a division of Penguin Books USA Inc.
375 Hudson Street, New York, New York 10014

Designed by Brenda van Ginkel
Produced by Somerville House Books Limited,
3080 Yonge Street, Suite 5000, Toronto, Ontario, Canada M4N 3N1

Printed in Hong Kong   First Edition
2 4 6 8 10 9 7 5 3 1

·TABLE OF CONTENTS·

A Safety Reminder

The recipes and activities in this book are for
adults and children to do together. Before you start, ask
your mom, dad, or another grown-up to help you.
Your grown-up helper can show you the safe way to take
things out of the oven, using oven mitts or pot holders.
Always be very careful when you are around a stove.
Never handle anything hot with your bare hands.

It's time to have some fun with numbers and shapes!

Here's what you'll need:

MIXING BOWLS

**COOKIE COUNT
MEASURING SPOONS**

MEASURING CUP

MIXING SPOON

**PLASTIC WRAP
OR WAXED PAPER**

ROLLING PIN

CRAFT SUPPLIES

**COOKIE COUNT
COOKIE SHEET**

**OVEN MITTS
OR POT HOLDERS**

**COOKIE COUNT
COOKIE CUTTERS**

SPATULA

·COUNT-THEM-OUT SUGAR COOKIES·

This is the basic recipe that all the different cookies
in this book start with. When you use the other recipes, you can
look back at these pictures to see how each step is done.

WHAT YOU NEED:

1/2 cup (125 mL or 1 stick) butter
    or margarine, softened
3/4 cup (175 mL) white sugar
1 egg
1 teaspoon (5 mL) vanilla extract

11/2 cups (375 mL) all-purpose flour
1/2 teaspoon (2 mL) baking powder
1/4 teaspoon (1 mL) salt
cooking spray or extra butter for
    greasing the cookie sheet
Cookie Count cutters

WHAT YOU DO:

1 Mix the butter and sugar together in a big bowl until they are creamy.

2 Add the egg and vanilla extract to the bowl. Mix again.

3 In another bowl, stir the flour, baking powder, and salt together.

4 Bit by bit, add the flour mixture to the bowl with the butter mixture and mix until smooth.

5 Pat the dough into a ball and wrap it in plastic wrap or waxed paper. Put the dough in the freezer for about 15 minutes.

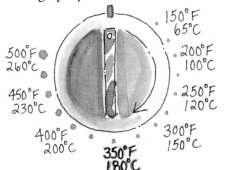

6 Preheat the oven to 350°F (180°C). Grease your cookie sheet with the cooking spray or extra butter.

150°F 65°C
200°F 100°C
500°F 260°C
450°F 230°C
250°F 120°C
400°F 200°C
300°F 150°C
350°F 180°C

7 Roll out the dough on a floured surface until it is half as thick as your cookie cutters. Cut out the dough, using any of the Cookie Count cookie cutters.

8 Gently remove the extra dough around the cutters. Put the cookies on your cookie sheet, leaving a space as wide as three of your fingers around each one.

9 Bake the cookies for about 10 to 12 minutes. Let the cookies cool before you eat them.

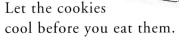

·NIBBLY NUMBERS·

Use the number cookie cutter(s) that match your age to make mint cookies just for you. Or make a batch of number cookies as a present for a friend's birthday. Just find out how old your friend will be and make lots of cookies out of that number!

WHAT YOU NEED:

1/2 cup (125 mL or 1 stick) butter or margarine, softened
3/4 cup (175 mL) white sugar
1 egg
several drops green or red food coloring

1 teaspoon (5 mL) mint extract
1 1/2 cups (375 mL) all-purpose flour
1/2 teaspoon (2 mL) baking powder
1/4 teaspoon (1 mL) salt
cooking spray or extra butter for greasing the cookie sheet
Cookie Count number cutters

WHAT YOU DO:

1 Mix the butter and sugar together in a big bowl until they are creamy.

2 Add the egg, food coloring, and mint extract to the bowl. Mix again.

3 In another bowl, stir the flour, baking powder, and salt together.

4 Bit by bit, add the flour mixture to the bowl with the butter mixture and mix until smooth.

5 Pat the dough into a ball and wrap it in plastic wrap or waxed paper. Put the dough in the freezer for about 15 minutes.

6 Preheat the oven to 350°F (180°C). Grease your cookie sheet with the cooking spray or extra butter.

7 Roll out the dough on a floured surface until it is half as thick as your cookie cutters. Cut out the dough, using the number cutter(s) that you have picked out.

8 Gently remove the extra dough around the cutters. Put the cookies on your cookie sheet, leaving a space as wide as three of your fingers around each one.

9 Bake the cookies for about 10 to 12 minutes. Let the cookies cool before you eat them.

What other special numbers do you have?
Find the cutters that match the numbers in:

YOUR PHONE NUMBER

YOUR SHOE SIZE

YOUR WEIGHT

YOUR ADDRESS

YOUR HEIGHT

· Try This ·

Before you bake the cookies, decorate each
one with chocolate chips. Match the number
of chocolate chips to the number of the cookie. Put two chocolate chips
on the 2 cookie, three chocolate chips on the 3 cookie, and so on.

·BAKE·A·SHAPE·

Make these orange-flavored cookies and discover
a delicious way to remember the number of sides on a triangle,
square, pentagon, and hexagon!

TRIANGLE

3 SIDES

SQUARE

4 SIDES

PENTAGON

5 SIDES

HEXAGON

6 SIDES

WHAT YOU NEED:

1/2 cup (125 mL or 1 stick) butter
    or margarine, softened

3/4 cup (175 mL) white sugar

1 egg

1 teaspoon (5 mL) vanilla or
    orange extract

2 teaspoons (10 mL) grated
    orange rind

1 1/2 cups (375 mL) all-purpose flour

1/2 teaspoon (2 mL) baking powder

1/4 teaspoon (1 mL) salt

cooking spray or extra butter for
    greasing the cookie sheet

miniature chocolate chips

Cookie Count shape cutters:
    small triangle, small square,
    pentagon, and hexagon

WHAT YOU DO:

1 Mix the butter and sugar together in a big bowl until they are creamy.

2 Add the egg, extract, and orange rind to the bowl. Mix again.

3 In another bowl, stir the flour, baking powder, and salt together.

4 Bit by bit, add the flour mixture to the bowl with the butter mixture and mix until smooth.

5 Pat the dough into a ball and wrap it in plastic wrap or waxed paper. Put the dough in the freezer for about 15 minutes.

6 Preheat the oven to 350°F (180°C). Grease your cookie sheet with the cooking spray or butter.

7 Roll out the dough on a floured surface until it is half as thick as your cutters. Cut out the dough, using the shape cutters.

8 Gently remove the extra dough around the cutters. Put the cookies on your cookie sheet, leaving a space as wide as three of your fingers around each one.

9 Count the number of sides each cookie has, then place the same number of chocolate chips on the cookie.

10 Bake the cookies for about 10 to 12 minutes. Let the cookies cool before you eat them.

13

·COCOA COOKIE QUILTS·

A quilt is a warm covering for a bed. It's often made
from pieces of fabric in different shapes that are sewn together.
You can make your own small cookie quilts — and find out how
big shapes are sometimes made up of several smaller shapes.

WHAT YOU NEED:

1/2 cup (125 mL or 1 stick) butter
or margarine, softened

3/4 cup (175 mL) white sugar

1 egg

1 teaspoon (5 mL) vanilla extract

1 1/2 cups (375 mL) all-purpose flour

1/2 teaspoon (2 mL) baking powder

1/4 teaspoon (1 mL) salt

2 tablespoons (25 mL) unsweetened
cocoa

cooking spray or extra butter for
greasing the cookie sheet

Cookie Count small square cutter

WHAT YOU DO:

1 Mix the butter and sugar together in a big bowl until they are creamy.

2 Add the egg and vanilla extract to the bowl. Mix again.

3 In another bowl, stir the flour, baking powder, and salt (but *not* the cocoa) together.

4 Bit by bit, add the flour mixture to the bowl with the butter mixture and mix until smooth.

5 Pat the dough into a ball, then divide it into two smaller balls, each the same size. Wrap one ball in plastic wrap or waxed paper. Put that dough in the freezer for about 15 minutes.

6 Put the other dough ball back in the bowl and sprinkle the cocoa on top. Knead the dough with your hands until the cocoa is blended in smoothly and the dough is brown.

7 Wrap the cocoa ball in plastic wrap or waxed paper. Put it in the freezer for about 15 minutes.

15

8 Preheat the oven to 350°F (180°C). Grease your cookie sheet with the cooking spray or extra butter.

9 Roll out the plain dough on a floured surface until it is half as thick as your cookie cutters. Cut out the dough, using the small square cutter. Do the same with the cocoa dough.

10 Gently remove the extra dough around the dough squares. Take two cocoa squares and two plain squares and place them together on your cookie sheet (as shown) to make a big square. Overlap the edges of the small squares slightly and press them so they stick together and bake in one piece. Be sure to leave a space as wide as three of your fingers around each quilt cookie.

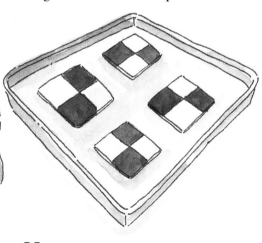

11 Bake the cookies for about 12 minutes. Let the cookies cool before you eat them.

·FESTIVE FUN·

Look at the shape cutters and at things around you.
What can you spot that is made of shapes? Use your cutters
to make cookies in the shapes of houses, trees, and other
things you see. Then arrange them to make a big picture. You
can also decorate the cookies with edible "paint"
(see page 19) before you bake them.

WHAT YOU NEED:

$1/2$ cup (125 mL or 1 stick) butter
or margarine, softened

$3/4$ cup (175 mL) white sugar

1 egg

1 teaspoon (5 mL) vanilla extract

$1^1/2$ cups (375 mL) all-purpose flour

$1/2$ teaspoon (2 mL) baking powder

$1/4$ teaspoon (1 mL) salt

cooking spray or extra butter for
greasing the cookie sheet

Cookie Count shape cutters

WHAT YOU DO:

1 To make the cookies, mix the butter and sugar together in a big bowl until they are creamy.

2 Add the egg and vanilla extract to the bowl. Mix again.

3 In another bowl, stir the flour, baking powder, and salt together.

4 Bit by bit, add the flour mixture to the bowl with the butter mixture and mix until smooth.

5 Pat the dough into a ball and wrap it in plastic wrap or waxed paper. Put the dough in the freezer for about 15 minutes.

6 Preheat the oven to 350°F (180°C). Grease your cookie sheet with the cooking spray or extra butter.

7 Roll out the dough on a floured surface until it is half as thick as your cookie cutters. Cut out the dough, using the shape cutters you need for your scene.

8 Gently remove the extra dough around the cutters. If you are making things for your picture that use more than one dough shape, overlap the edges of the small dough shapes slightly and press them so they stick together and bake in one piece. Put the cookies on your cookie sheet, leaving a space as wide as three of your fingers around each one.

9 Bake the cookies for about 10 to 12 minutes. Let the cookies cool and then arrange them to make a picture on your clean cookie sheet. If you want a snowy scene, decorate your cookies with white icing and place white paper on the sheet before you put the cookies down on it.

•FOR MORE FUN•

Make some "paint" and color your cookies *before* you bake them! In a small dish, beat together an egg yolk, a few drops of water, and some food coloring. If you want paint in other colors, use another egg yolk and different food coloring. (Do not eat this "paint" until it has been baked.) Dab the paint on the cookies, using a cotton swab. Then bake and enjoy.

·COOKIE COUNT PARTY·

For your next birthday party, make a cookie treasure chest and fill it with cookie numbers. At the party, play a numbers game with your guests, and serve up Easy 1, 2, 3 Chocolate Milk and Tasty Number Sandwiches.

·A COOKIE TREASURE CHEST·

WHAT YOU NEED:

For the treasure chest and the cookies

2 batches of dough from your favorite cookie recipe in this book to make the treasure chest (it's easier to make one batch at a time rather than doubling the ingredients)

1 batch of dough from another cookie recipe in this book to make the numbers

large flat plate or other base for your treasure chest

Cookie Count number cutters and large rectangle cutter

For the icing

1 egg white

1 1/2 to 2 cups (375 to 500 mL) powdered sugar

1/4 teaspoon (1 mL) cream of tartar

raisins, sunflower seeds, sprinkles, or tiny candies for decoration

WHAT YOU DO:

1 Make the two batches of dough you have chosen for the treasure chest.

2 Using the large rectangle cutter, cut out six rectangles—four for the sides of the treasure chest, and two for the lid. (If you have any leftover dough, you can use it to make some extra number cookies.)

3 Place two rectangles at a time on the cookie sheet, leaving a space as wide as three of your fingers between them. Bake each pair at 350°F (180°C) for 12 minutes.

4 While the treasure-chest pieces are cooling, make some number cookies by following the recipe you have chosen.

5 To make the icing for building the treasure chest, first put the egg white in a clean, grease-free bowl.

6 Bit by bit, stir in 3/4 cup (175 mL) powdered sugar and the cream of tartar. Mix until smooth.

7 Continue adding more sugar, bit by bit, stirring well all the time. When the icing sticks together and forms a stiff ball, it is ready to use. (You may not have to add all the sugar.) Be sure to use the icing right away, or it will harden.

8 Pinch off a piece of icing and roll it between your fingers to make a snake as wide as your thumb. Using your fingers, press the icing snake onto the long edge of one of the cookie rectangles.

9 Press the rectangle, icing edge down, onto the large plate. Make sure you leave enough space on the plate for the other sides to fit. Hold the rectangle there for 30 seconds or until the icing sets a little. This is the first side of your treasure chest.

10 Roll another icing snake, and press it onto the long edge of another cookie rectangle.

11 Press the rectangle, icing edge down, onto the plate at a right angle to the first side. Hold the new rectangle in place for 30 seconds.

This is the second side of your treasure chest.

12 Where the two rectangles join, fill in the corner with an icing snake on the outside and another on the inside. Press the corners together for 30 seconds.

13 Repeat steps 8-12 to form the third and fourth sides of your chest.

Be sure to fill in all four corners with icing.

14 You now have two cookie rectangles left for the lid. Roll an icing snake and press it onto the long edge of one of the rectangles. Press the long edge of the other rectangle flat against it. Hold the rectangles pressed together for several minutes while the icing dries. (Don't lay the lid down on a plate or table before the icing is dry, or the lid might stick to that surface.)

15 Use any leftover icing to fasten raisins, sunflower seeds, sprinkles, or tiny candies to the outside of the chest. You can also decorate the lid, if you like.

16 After the icing has hardened, fill your treasure chest with the number cookies. Carefully place the lid diagonally on top of the box. Now you're ready to play the Treasure Chest Numbers Game.

·EASY 1, 2, 3 CHOCOLATE MILK·

Use your measuring spoons to mix up party fun!

WHAT YOU NEED:

**1 glass of milk for each guest
chocolate syrup**

WHAT YOU DO:

1 Measure 1 to 2 tablespoons (15 to 25 mL) of chocolate syrup into each glass of milk.

2 Stir with a spoon.

3 Serve to your guests.

·How to Play the Treasure Chest Numbers Game·

Can you and your friends recognize numbers without actually looking at them? Here's one way to find out! Fill a bowl with the clean number cutters. Blindfold each guest in turn and ask the person to pick a cutter. If the person can tell what the number is without peeking, open up your treasure chest and give him or her the matching number cookie as a prize!

·TASTY NUMBER SANDWICHES·

**Before you bite into these sandwiches,
look for the outlines of the numbers on top!**

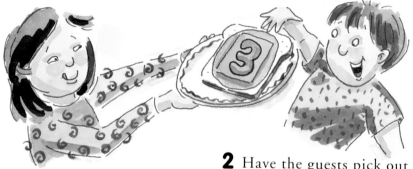

WHAT YOU NEED:

1 plate for each guest
1 square slice of cheese for each guest
1 slice of bread for each guest
1 slice of bologna or ham for each
   guest
Cookie Count number cutters

WHAT YOU DO:

1 Place a cheese slice on each guest's plate.

2 Have the guests pick out their favorite number cutter, then press it into the slice of cheese. They should then carefully lift the cutter, removing the number shape from the cheese square.

3 Pass a slice of bread and a slice of meat to each of your guests. Have them place the meat on the bread, then cover it with their cheese square. They should be able to see the outline of their numbers on their sandwiches!

·CONCENTRATION GAME·

This play dough can be baked, but not eaten. Use it to make your very own reusable number game. Then ask a friend to play with you, and see how well you remember your numbers!

WHAT YOU NEED:

4 cups (1000 mL) all-purpose flour
1 cup (250 mL) salt
1 1/2 cups (375 mL) warm water
large piece of felt or construction paper
nontoxic white glue
nontoxic poster paint
Cookie Count number cutters and large circle cutter

WHAT YOU DO:

1 Preheat the oven to 300°F (150°C).

2 Mix the flour and salt together.

3 Add the water and mix well with your hands.

4 Roll out the dough until it is half as thick as your cookie cutters. Using the large circle cutter, cut out 20 circles.

5 Gently remove the extra dough around the dough circles. Put the circles on your cookie sheet, leaving a space as wide as three of your fingers around each circle.

6 Press the zero cutter gently into the middle of one dough circle so that the zero leaves a mark, but does not cut all the way through the dough. (If you make a mistake, just squeeze the dough together, roll it out again, and start over.) Do this again with the same cutter on another circle.

7 Repeat with the other number cutters, making sure that you mark each number on two dough circles.

8 Bake in the oven for about one hour. Let the circles cool.

9 With a pencil, trace around the large circle cutter 20 times on the felt or construction paper.

10 Cut out the felt or paper circles. Ask a grown-up to help you if you are cutting out felt.

11 Match a felt or paper circle with each dough circle. Glue one felt or paper circle to the back of each dough circle (the side without the number on it).

12 If you like, highlight the numbers on the dough circles with paint.

·How to Play Concentration·

1 Jumble the circles and place them on a table, with the numbers facing down.

2 The first player turns over two circles. If the numbers match, the player keeps the circles. If the numbers don't match, the player turns the circles back over, leaving them in the same place. Each player tries to remember which numbers are on the circles before they are turned back over.

3 The next player takes a turn.

4 Play until all the circles are matched up. The player with the most circles is the winner!

·CLEAN-UP FUN·

What's the next best thing to making cookies?
Washing up when you are done!

WHAT YOU NEED:

dishpan or sink
water
food coloring (blue works best)
dirty mixing bowls, measuring
**   cup, and measuring spoons**
dishwashing liquid

WHAT YOU DO:

1 Ask your grown-up helper to fill the dishpan or sink with water.

2 Add several drops of food coloring to the water and stir. (The food coloring will make the water easier to see.)

3 Carefully add the dirty bowls, cup, and spoons to the water. (Make sure that no dishes are breakable.)

4 Now have some fun! Count the number of teaspoons of water it takes to fill one tablespoon. Pour water from the tablespoon into the measuring cup and see how many spoonfuls you need to fill the cup. Then pour the full measuring cup into one of the empty mixing bowls. How many more cups of water do you have to add to fill the bowl?

5 When you are finished measuring and pouring, ask a grown-up to help you wash, rinse, and dry the cutters, cookie sheet, bowls, cup, and spoons.

6 Match up the different bowls, measuring spoons, and cookie cutters, and put them away, so everything will be easy to find the next time you bake!

·NUMBERS AND SHAPES EVERYWHERE·

Can you find the numbers from 0 to 9 in this picture?
How many Cookie Count shapes
can you see?

·MORE THINGS YOU CAN DO WITH YOUR COOKIE COUNT CUTTERS·

Play with them in the snow or at the beach!

Create a cookie clock by baking a big round cookie in a pizza pan. Then place number cookies around your clock, sticking them on with icing!

Trace the shape cutters on construction paper. Then cut out the shapes and punch two holes in each one. Run a long string through the holes, then hang up your paper-shape banner.

Make delicious gelatin shapes. Ask a grown-up to make some extra-firm gelatin. After it has chilled, use your cutters to make some cool shapes.

* Be sure to wash your cookie cutters right away so they're ready when you want to bake cookies again!